The Pictorial Bible, Vol. 1:
The Pentateuch

To My Wife, kids and our church family

The Pictorial Bible Vol. I
The Pentateuch

By Fred DeRuvo

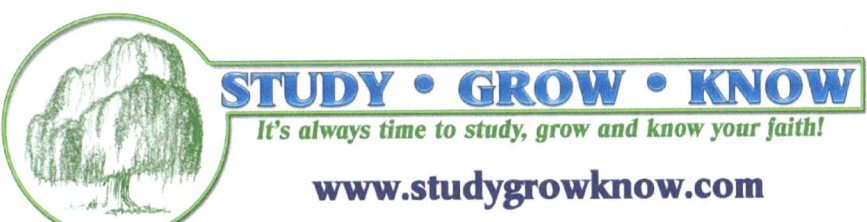

www.studygrowknow.com

Copyright © 2009 by Study-Grow-Know

All rights reserved. Written permission must be secured from the publisher to use or reproduce any part of this book, except brief quotations in critical reviews or articles.

Published in Scotts Valley, California, by Study-Grow-Know
www.studygrowknow.com • www.rightly-dividing.com

Scripture quoted by permission. Quotations are from the NET Bible® (unless otherwise noted), copyright ©1996-2006 by Biblical Studies Press, L.L.C. www.bible.org All rights reserved.

Images used in this publication (unless otherwise noted) are from clipartconnection.com and used with permission, ©2007 JUPITERIMAGES, and its licensors. All rights reserved.

All Woodcuts used herein are in the Public Domain and free of copyright.

All Figure illustrations used in this book were created by the author and protected under copyright laws, © 2009.

Library of Congress Cataloging-in-Publication Data

DeRuvo, Fred, 1957 –

ISBN 0977424472
EAN-13 9780977424474

1. Religion – Biblical Theology – Apologetics

Foreword

I have always learned best through the visual process. I enjoy reading, but I am able to pick something up much more quickly by seeing a demonstration of it, or by associated pictures with the information.

During the process of refreshing my memory about certain events in the Bible, it dawned on me that there are undoubtedly others who learn like I do. Because of that, I began to think of ways to make the Bible come alive for folks who rely on visual cues, along with text.

It was not too long before I came up with the idea of creating an outline for each book of the Bible, based on existing chapters. If folks could learn one concept from each chapter, and tie that concept in with an illustration, then it would probably be a great deal easier for people to gain an overall understanding and appreciation for God's Word.

I realized that this would be, of necessity, a starting point and that's all I wanted it to be. If people could get this "starting point" under their belt, adding to it would be easy.

And the Pictorial Outline Bible was born! Welcome to the first in the series, of which I hope to have the entire Bible completed in the not-too-distant future. This first book, contains the first five books of the Bible, commonly referred to as the Pentateuch. You'll note that in general, there are four parts on each page, representing one chapter for each part. You'll also quickly discover that the entire book is color formatted, because that helps with the memory process. Colors stand out, enriching the information.

I hope you enjoy this work, and I invite your comments. Be on the lookout for the next in the series! Stay tuned to our website for the latest up to date information about this, and all of my other books at:

www.studygrowknow.com

- Fred DeRuvo – September, 2009

Contents

Section 1:	Genesis 7

Section 2:	Exodus 21

Section 3:	Leviticus 32

Section 4:	Numbers 40

Section 5:	Deuteronomy 50

Notes & List of Resources 60

Section 1

Genesis:
Book of Beginnings

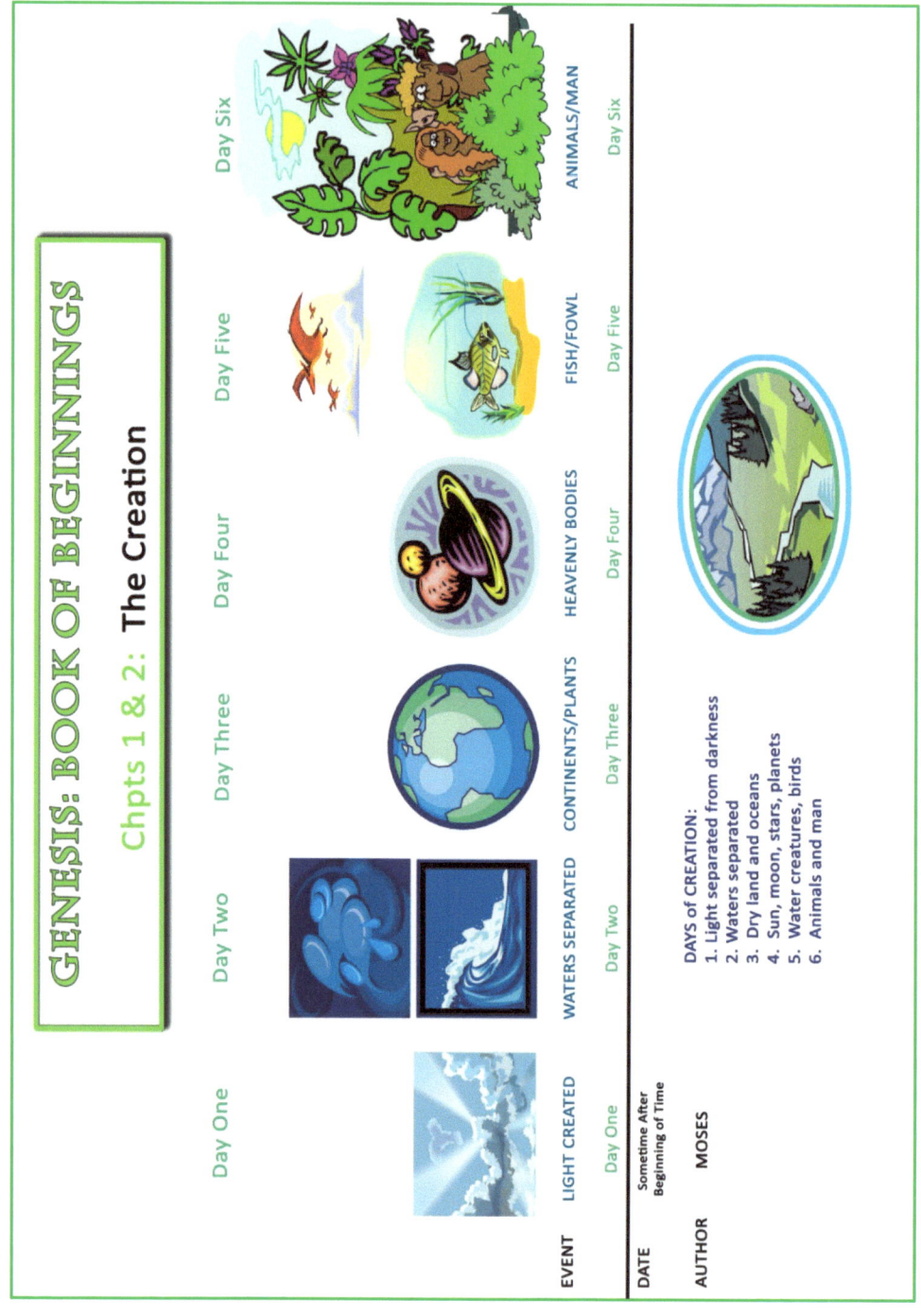

GENESIS: BOOK OF BEGINNINGS

Chpt 3: The Fall

"Behold, the man has become like one of Us, to know good and evil. And now, lest he put out his hand and take also of the tree of life, and eat, and live forever" – there the LORD God sent him out of the garden of Eden to till the ground from which he was taken. So He drove out the man; and He placed cherubim at the east of the garden of Eden, and a flaming sword which turned every way, to guard the way to the tree of life."
Genesis 3:22-24

Chpt 4: Can Murders Abel

"And the Lord respected Abel and his offering, but He did not respect Cain and his offering. And Cain was very angry; and his countenance fell...now Cain talked with Abel his brother; and it came to pass, when they were in the field, that Cain rose up against Abel his brother and killed him."
Genesis 4:4b-5

Chpt 5: From Adam to Noah

Adam (930 yrs) - Seth (912 yrs) - Enosh (905 yrs) - Kenan (910 yrs) - Mahalalel (895 yrs) - Jared (962 yrs) - Enoch (365 yrs+) - Methuselah (969 yrs) - Lamech (777 yrs) - *Noah*

Chpt 6: The Wickedness of Man

"Then the Lord saw that the wickedness of man was great in the earth, and that every intent of the thoughts of his heart was only evil continually."
Genesis 6:5

Chpt 7: The Great Flood

"And it came to pass after seven days that the waters of the flood were on the earth. In the six hundredth year of Noah's life, in the second month, the seventeenth day of the month, on that day all the fountains of the great deep were broken up, and the windows of the heaven were opened. And the rain was on the earth for forty days and forty nights."
Genesis 7:10-12

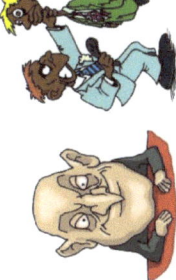

GENESIS: BOOK OF BEGINNINGS

Chpt 8: God's Covenant w/Creation

"(Noah) offered burnt offerings on the altar. And the Lord smelled a soothing aroma. Then the Lord said in His heart 'I will never again curse the ground for man's sake'..." Genesis 8:20-21-10

Chpt 9: Starting Over

"Behold, I will establish My covenant with you and with your descendants after you, and with every living creature that is with you..." Genesis 9:9-10

Chpt 10: Nations Descended

"Now this is the geneaology of the sons of Noah: Shem, Ham and Japheth. And sons were born to them after the flood." Genesis 10:1

Chpt 11: Tower of Babel

"Now the whole earth had one language and one speech...but the Lord came down to see the city and the tower which the sons of men had built...so the Lord scattered them abroad from there over the face of all the earth and they ceased building the city." Genesis 11:1, 5, 8

GENESIS: BOOK OF BEGINNINGS

Chpt 12: Promises to Abram

"Now the Lord had said to Abram: 'Get out of your country, from your family and from your father's house, to a land that I will show you. I will make you a great nation; I will bless you and make your name great; and you shall be a blessing. I will bless those who bless you, and I will curse him who curses you; and in you all the families of the earth shall be blessed'."
Genesis 12:1-3

Chpt 13: Abram Inherits Canaan

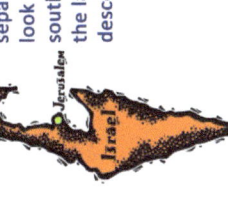

"And the Lord said to Abram, after Lot had separated from him: "Lift your eyes now and look from the place where you are – northward, southward, eastward, and westward; for all the land which you see I give to you and your descendants forever'." Genesis 13:14-15

Chpt 14: Lots' Captivity and Rescue

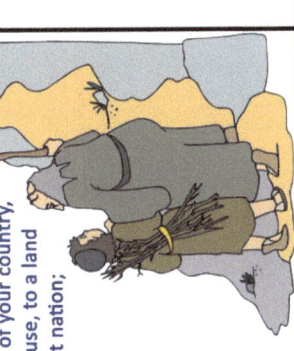

"When Abram heard that his nephew had been taken captive, he mobilized his trained men who had been born in his household, and he pursued the invaders as far as Dan. Then, during the night, Abram divided his forces against them and defeated them. He chased them as far as Hobah, which is north of Damascus. He retrieved all the stolen property. He also brought back his nephew Lot and his possessions, as well as the women and the rest of the people."
Genesis 14:14-16

Chpt 15: Abrahamic Covenant

"...a son who comes from your own body will be your heir." The Lord took him outside and said, "Gaze into the sky and count the stars – if you are able to count them!" Then he said to him, "So will your descendants be."
Genesis 15:4b-5

GENESIS: BOOK OF BEGINNINGS

Chpt 16: Hagar and Ishmael

"Now Sarai, Abram's wife, had not given birth to any children, but she had an Egyptian servant named Hagar. So Sarai said to Abram, "Since the Lord has prevented me from having children, have sexual relations with my servant. Perhaps I can have a family by her." Abram did what Sarai told him. So after Abram had lived in Canaan for ten years, Sarai, Abram's wife, gave Hagar, her Egyptian servant, to her husband to be his wife. He had sexual relations with Hagar, and she became pregnant. Once Hagar realized she was pregnant, she despised Sarai." Genesis 16:1-4

Chpt 17: Sign of Circumcision

This is my requirement that you and your descendants after you must keep: Every male among you must be circumcised. You must circumcise the flesh of your foreskins. This will be a reminder of the covenant between me and you. Throughout your generations every male among you who is eight days old must be circumcised, whether born in your house or bought with money from any foreigner who is not one of your descendants." Genesis 17:10-12

Chpt 18: Three Visitors to Abraham

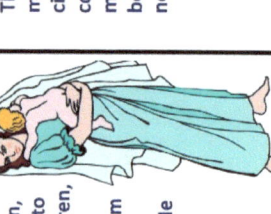

The Lord said to Abraham, "Why did Sarah laugh and say, 'Will I really have a child when I am old?' Is anything impossible for the Lord? I will return to you when the season comes round again and Sarah will have a son." Then Sarah lied, saying, "I did not laugh," because she was afraid. But the Lord said, "No! You did laugh."
Genesis 18:13-15

Chpt 19: Sodom and Gomorrah

The sun had just risen over the land as Lot reached Zoar. Then the Lord rained down sulfur and fire on Sodom and Gomorrah. It was sent down from the sky by the Lord. So he overthrew those cities and all that region, including all the inhabitants of the cities and the vegetation that grew from the ground. But Lot's wife looked back longingly and was turned into a pillar of salt. Genesis 19:23-26

GENESIS: BOOK OF BEGINNINGS

Chpt 20: Abraham Lies About Sarah

Abraham journeyed from there to the Negev region and settled between Kadesh and Shur. While he lived as a temporary resident in Gerar, Abraham said about his wife Sarah, "She is my sister." So Abimelech, king of Gerar, sent for Sarah and took her. Genesis 20:1-2

Chpt 21: Isaac is Born

The Lord visited Sarah just as he had said he would and did for Sarah what he had promised. So Sarah became pregnant and bore Abraham a son in his old age at the appointed time that God had told him. Abraham named his son — whom Sarah bore to him — Isaac. When his son Isaac was eight days old, Abraham circumcised him just as God had commanded him to do. (Now Abraham was a hundred years old when his son Isaac was born to him.) Genesis 21:1-5

Chpt 22: Sacrifice of Isaac

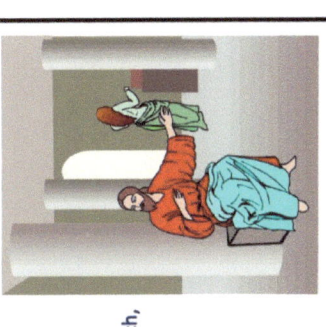

Some time after these things God tested Abraham. He said to him, "Abraham!" "Here I am!" Abraham replied. God said, "Take your son — your only son, whom you love, Isaac — and go to the land of Moriah! Offer him up there as a burnt offering on one of the mountains which I will indicate to you."

Genesis 22:1-2

Chpt 23: Death of Sarah

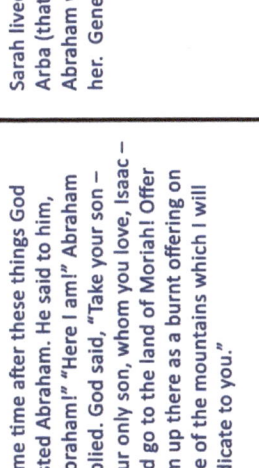

Sarah lived 127 years. Then she died in Kiriath Arba (that is, Hebron) in the land of Canaan. Abraham went to mourn for Sarah and to weep for her. Genesis 23:1-2

GENESIS: BOOK OF BEGINNINGS

Chpt 24: A Wife for Isaac

Now Abraham was old, well advanced in years, and the Lord had blessed him in everything. Abraham said to his servant, the senior one in his household who was in charge of everything he had, "Put your hand under my thigh so that I may make you solemnly promise by the Lord, the God of heaven and the God of the earth: You must not acquire a wife for my son from the daughters of the Canaanites, among whom I am living. You must go instead to my country and to my relatives to find a wife for my son Isaac." Genesis 24:1-4

Chpt 25: Death of Abraham, Sons of Ishmael, Jacob & Esau

Abraham lived a total of years. Then Abraham breathed his last and died at a good old age, an old man who had lived a full life. He joined his ancestors. Genesis 25:7-8

This is the account of Abraham's son Ishmael, whom Hagar the Egyptian, Sarah's servant, bore to Abraham. Genesis 25:12

"Two nations are in your womb, and two peoples will be separated from within you. One people will be stronger than the other, and the older will serve the younger." Genesis 25:23

Chpt 26: Isaac Lies About His Wife

When the men of that place asked him about his wife, he replied, "She is my sister." He was afraid to say, "She is my wife," for he thought to himself, "The men of this place will kill me to get Rebekah because she is very beautiful." Genesis 26:7

Chpt 27: Jacob Cheats Esau

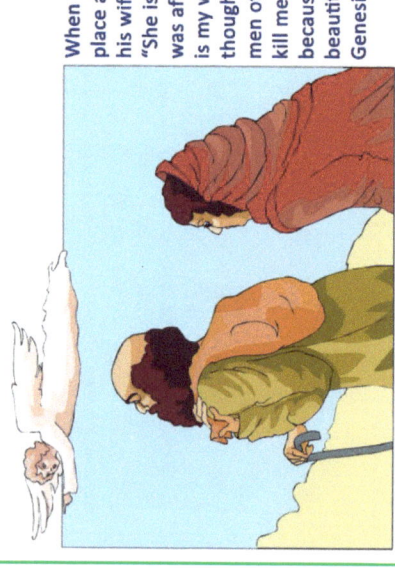

Then Rebekah took her older son Esau's best clothes, which she had with her in the house, and put them on her younger son Jacob. She put the skins of the young goats on his hands and the smooth part of his neck. Then she handed the tasty food and the bread she had made to her son Jacob. Genesis 27:15-17

GENESIS: BOOK OF BEGINNINGS

Chpt 28: Jacob's Dream

[Jacob] fell asleep in that place and had a dream. He saw a stairway erected on the earth with its top reaching to the heavens. The angels of God were going up and coming down it and the Lord stood at its top. He said, "I am the Lord, the God of your grandfather Abraham and the God of your father Isaac. I will give you and your descendants the ground you are lying on. Your descendants will be like the dust of the earth, and you will spread out to the west, east, north, and south...I am with you! I will protect you wherever you go and will bring you back to this land. I will not leave you until I have done what I promised you!" Genesis 28:11b-15

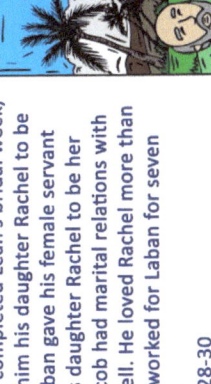

Chpt 29: Marriages of Jacob

When Jacob completed Leah's bridal week, Laban gave him his daughter Rachel to be his wife. (Laban gave his female servant Bilhah to his daughter Rachel to be her servant.) Jacob had marital relations with Rachel as well. He loved Rachel more than Leah, so he worked for Laban for seven more years.
Genesis 29:28-30

Chpt 30: Jacob's Family and Flocks

In this way Jacob became extremely prosperous. He owned large flocks, male and female servants, camels, and donkeys.
Genesis 30:43

Chpt 31: Jacob Flees from Laban

Jacob heard that Laban's sons were complaining, "Jacob has taken everything that belonged to our father! He has gotten rich at our father's expense!" When Jacob saw the look on Laban's face, he could tell his attitude toward him had changed. The Lord said to Jacob, "Return to the land of your fathers and to your relatives. I will be with you."
Genesis 31:1-3

GENESIS: BOOK OF BEGINNINGS

Chpt 32: Jacob Wrestles with God

Then the man said, "Let me go, for the dawn is breaking." "I will not let you go," Jacob replied, "unless you bless me." The man asked him, "What is your name?" He answered, "Jacob." "No longer will your name be Jacob," the man told him, "but Israel, because you have fought with God and with men and have prevailed. Genesis 32:26-28

Chpt 33: Jacob Meets Esau

Jacob looked up and saw that Esau was coming along with four hundred men. So he divided the children among Leah, Rachel, and the two female servants. He put the servants and their children in front, with Leah and her children behind them, and Rachel and Joseph behind them. But Jacob himself went on ahead of them, and he bowed toward the ground seven times as he approached his brother. But Esau ran to meet him, embraced him, hugged his neck, and kissed him. Then they both wept. Genesis 33:1-4

Chpt 34: Dinah & the Shechemites

They killed Hamor and his son Shechem with the sword, took Dinah from Shechem's house, and left. Jacob's sons killed them and looted the city because their sister had been violated. They took their flocks, herds, and donkeys, as well as everything in the city and in the surrounding fields. They captured as plunder all their wealth, all their little ones, and their wives, including everything in the houses. Genesis 34:26-29

Chpt 35: Jacob Returns to Bethel

Then God said to Jacob, "Go up at once to Bethel and live there. Make an altar there to God, who appeared to you when you fled from your brother Esau." So Jacob told his household and all who were with him, "Get rid of the foreign gods you have among you. Purify yourselves and change your clothes. Let us go up at once to Bethel. Then I will make an altar there to God, who responded to me in my time of distress and has been with me wherever I went. Genesis 35:1-3

GENESIS: BOOK OF BEGINNINGS

Chpt 36: Descendants of Esau

This is the account of Esau, the father of the Edomites, in the hill country of Seir. These were the names of Esau's sons:
Eliphaz, the son of Esau's wife Adah, and Reuel, the son of Esau's wife Basemath.

The sons of Eliphaz were:
Teman, Omar, Zepho, Gatam, and Kenaz

Genesis 36:9-11

Chpt 37: Joseph's Dreams & Slavery

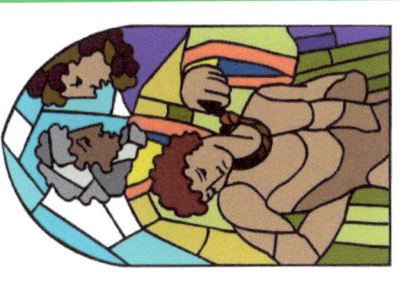

Now Israel loved Joseph more than all his sons because he was a son born to him late in life, and he made a special tunic for him. When Joseph's brothers saw that their father loved him more than any of them, they hated Joseph and were not able to speak to him kindly. Joseph had a dream, and when he told his brothers about it, they hated him even more.

Genesis 37:3-5

Chpt 38: Judah and Tamar

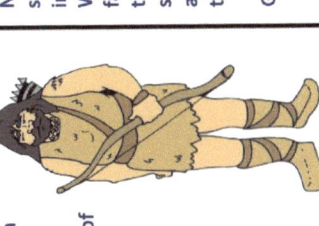

Then Judah said to Onan, "Have sexual relations with your brother's wife and fulfill the duty of a brother-in-law to her so that you may raise up a descendant for your brother." But Onan knew that the child would not be considered his. So whenever he had sexual relations with his brother's wife, he withdrew prematurely so as not to give his brother a descendant. What he did was evil in the Lord's sight, so the Lord killed him too.
Genesis 38:8-10

Chpt 39: Joseph and Potiphar's Wife

When his master heard his wife say, "This is the way your slave treated me," he became furious. Joseph's master took him and threw him into the prison, the place where the king's prisoners were confined. So he was there in the prison. But the Lord was with Joseph and showed him kindness. He granted him favor in the sight of the prison warden.
Genesis 39:19-21

GENESIS: BOOK OF BEGINNINGS

Chpt 40: Cupbearer and the Baker

After these things happened, the cupbearer to the king of Egypt and the royal baker offended their master, the king of Egypt. Pharaoh was enraged with his two officials, the cupbearer and the baker, so he imprisoned them in the house of the captain of the guard in the same facility where Joseph was confined. The captain of the guard appointed Joseph to be their attendant, and he served them.

Genesis 40:1-4

Chpt 41: Joseph's Rise to Power

So Pharaoh said to Joseph, "Because God has enabled you to know all this, there is no one as wise and discerning as you are! You will oversee my household, and all my people will submit to your commands. Only I, the king, will be greater than you.

Genesis 41:39-40

Chpt 42: Joseph's Brothers in Egypt

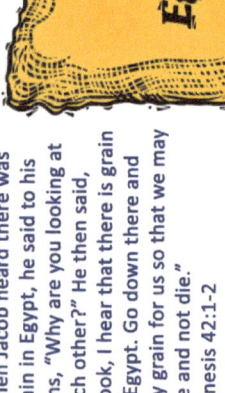

When Jacob heard there was grain in Egypt, he said to his sons, "Why are you looking at each other?" He then said, "Look, I hear that there is grain in Egypt. Go down there and buy grain for us so that we may live and not die."
Genesis 42:1-2

Chpt 43: Second Journey to Egypt

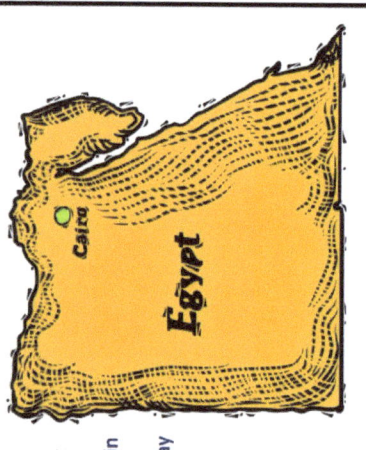

Now the famine was severe in the land. When they finished eating the grain they had brought from Egypt, their father said to them, "Return, buy us a little more food." But Judah said to him, "The man solemnly warned us, 'You will not see my face unless your brother is with you.' If you send our brother with us, we'll go down and buy food for you. But if you will not send him, we won't go down there because the man said to us, 'You will not see my face unless your brother is with you.'" Genesis 43:1-5

GENESIS: BOOK OF BEGINNINGS

Chpt 44: Joseph Tests His Brothers

He instructed the servant who was over his household, "Fill the sacks of the men with as much food as they can carry and put each man's money in the mouth of his sack. Then put my cup – the silver cup – in the mouth of the youngest one's sack, along with the money for his grain." He did as Joseph instructed.

Genesis 44:1-2

Chpt 45: Joseph Reconciles

Joseph was no longer able to control himself before all his attendants, so he cried out, "Make everyone go out from my presence!" No one remained with Joseph when he made himself known to his brothers. He wept loudly; the Egyptians heard it and Pharaoh's household heard about it. Joseph said to his brothers, "I am Joseph! Is my father still alive?" His brothers could not answer him because they were dumbfounded before him.

Genesis 45:1-3

Chpt 46: Jacob Moves to Egypt

So Israel began his journey, taking with him all that he had. When he came to Beer Sheba he offered sacrifices to the God of his father Isaac. God spoke to Israel in a vision during the night and said, "Jacob, Jacob!" He replied, "Here I am!" He said, "I am God, the God of your father. Do not be afraid to go down to Egypt, for I will make you into a great nation there. I will go down with you to Egypt and I myself will certainly bring you back from there. Joseph will close your eyes."
Genesis 46:1-4

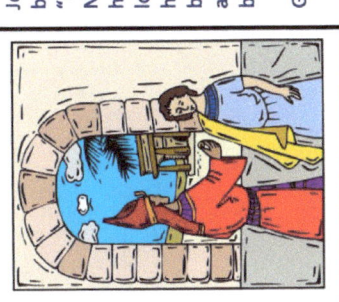

Chpt 47: Joseph Rules Wisely

Joseph said to the people, "Since I have bought you and your land today for Pharaoh, here is seed for you. Cultivate the land. When you gather in the crop, give one-fifth of it to Pharaoh, and the rest will be yours for seed for the fields and for you to eat, including those in your households and your little children."

They replied, "You have saved our lives! You are showing us favor, and we will be Pharaoh's slaves."
Genesis 47:23-25

GENESIS: BOOK OF BEGINNINGS

Chpt 48: Manasseh and Ephraim

So Joseph moved them from Israel's knees and bowed down with his face to the ground. Joseph positioned them; he put Ephraim on his right hand across from Israel's left hand, and Manasseh on his left hand across from Israel's right hand. Then Joseph brought them closer to his father. Israel stretched out his right hand and placed it on Ephraim's head, although he was the younger. Crossing his hands, he put his left hand on Manasseh's head, for Manasseh was the firstborn.

Genesis 48:12-14

Chpt 49: Joseph Blesses and Dies

These are the twelve tribes of Israel. This is what their father said to them when he blessed them. He gave each of them an appropriate blessing...When Jacob finished giving these instructions to his sons, he pulled his feet up onto the bed, breathed his last breath, and went to his people.

Genesis 49:28, 33

Chpt 50: Burials of Jacob and Joseph

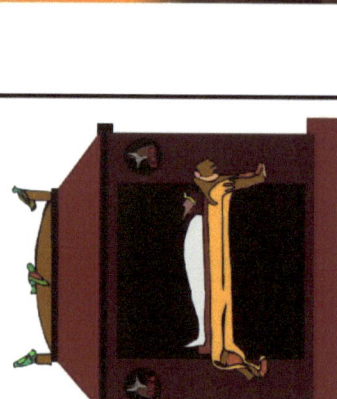

So Joseph went up to bury his father; all Pharaoh's officials went with him – the senior courtiers of his household, all the senior officials of the land of Egypt, all Joseph's household, his brothers, and his father's household...So Joseph died at the age of After they embalmed him, his body was placed in a coffin in Egypt.
Genesis 50:7-8, 26

~ End of Genesis ~

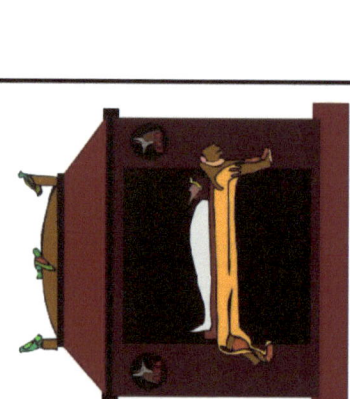

Section 2

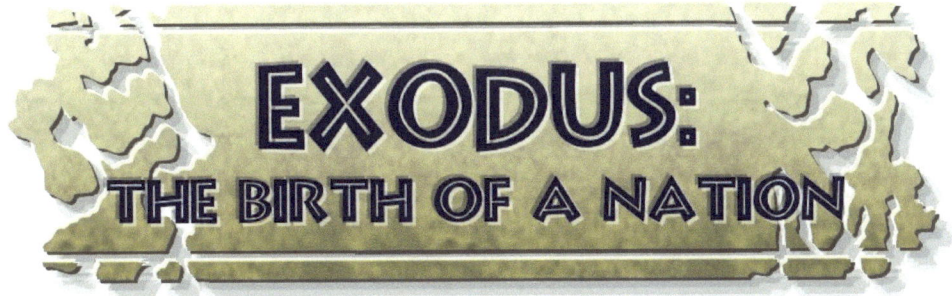

Exodus: The Birth of a Nation

Chpt 1: Blessing and Bondage in Egypt

Then a new king, who did not know about Joseph, came to power over Egypt. He said to his people, "Look at the Israelite people, more numerous and stronger than we are! Come, let's deal wisely with them. Otherwise they will continue to multiply, and if a war breaks out, they will ally themselves with our enemies and fight against us and leave the country."
Exodus 1:8-10

Chpt 2: Birth of the Deliverer

A man from the household of Levi married a woman who was a descendant of Levi. The woman became pregnant and gave birth to a son. When she saw that he was a healthy child, she hid him for three months. But when she was no longer able to hide him, she took a papyrus basket for him and sealed it with bitumen and pitch. She put the child in it and set it among the reeds along the edge of the Nile. His sister stationed herself at a distance to find out what would happen to him. Then the daughter of Pharaoh came down to wash herself by the Nile.... Exodus 2:1-5a

Chpt 3: The Burning Bush

Now Moses was shepherding the flock of his father-in-law Jethro, the priest of Midian, and he led the flock to the far side of the desert and came to the mountain of God, to Horeb. The angel of the Lord appeared to him in a flame of fire from within a bush. He looked – and the bush was ablaze with fire, but it was not being consumed!
Exodus 3:1-2

Chpt 4: God is All Sufficient

Lord said to him, "What is that in your hand?" He said, "A staff." The Lord said, "Throw it to the ground." So he threw it to the ground, and it became a snake, and Moses ran from it. But the Lord said to Moses, "Put out your hand and grab it by the tail" – so he put out his hand and caught it, and it became a staff in his hand...
Exodus 4:2-4

Exodus: The Birth of a Nation

Chpt 5: Pharaoh Opposes Moses

Afterward Moses and Aaron went to Pharaoh and said, "Thus says the Lord, the God of Israel, 'Release my people so that they may hold a pilgrim feast to me in the desert.'" But Pharaoh said, "Who is the Lord that I should obey him by releasing Israel? I do not know the Lord, and I will not release Israel!" Exodus 5:1-2

Chpt 6: God Charges Moses

Then the Lord said to Moses, "Go, tell Pharaoh king of Egypt that he must release the Israelites from his land." But Moses replied to the Lord, "If the Israelites did not listen to me, then how will Pharaoh listen to me, since I speak with difficulty?" The Lord spoke to Moses and Aaron and gave them a charge for the Israelites and Pharaoh king of Egypt to bring the Israelites out of the land of Egypt. Exodus 6:9-13

Chpt 7: Water to Blood

Then the Lord said to Moses, "Tell Aaron, 'Take your staff and stretch out your hand over Egypt's waters – over their rivers, over their canals, over their ponds, and over all their reservoirs – so that it becomes blood.' There will be blood everywhere in the land of Egypt, even in wooden and stone containers." Exodus 7:19

Chpt 8: Frogs, Gnats and Flies

The Nile will swarm with frogs, and they will come up and go into your house, in your bedroom, and on your bed, and into the houses of your servants and your people, and into your ovens and your kneading troughs. Frogs will come up against you, your people, and all your servants.'"

The Lord said to Moses, "Tell Aaron, 'Extend your staff and strike the dust of the ground, and it will become gnats throughout all the land of Egypt.

If you do not release my people, then I am going to send swarms of flies on you and on your servants and on your people and in your houses. The houses of the Egyptians will be full of flies, and even the ground they stand on." Exodus 8:3-4, 16, 21

Exodus: The Birth of a Nation

Chpt 9: Disease, Boils and Hail

the hand of the Lord will surely bring a very terrible plague on your livestock in the field, on the horses, the donkeys, the camels, the herds, and the flocks.

"Take handfuls of soot from a furnace, and have Moses throw it into the air while Pharaoh is watching. It will become fine dust over the whole land of Egypt and will cause boils to break out and fester on both people and animals in all the land of Egypt."

I am going to cause very severe hail to rain down about this time tomorrow, such hail as has never occurred in Egypt from the day it was founded until now. Exodus 9:3, 8-9, ,18

Chpt 10: Locusts and Darkness

But if you refuse to release my people, I am going to bring locusts into your territory tomorrow. They will cover the surface of the earth, so that you will be unable to see the ground. They will eat the remainder of what escaped – what is left over for you – from the hail, and they will eat every tree that grows for you from the field.

"Extend your hand toward heaven so that there may be darkness over the land of Egypt, a darkness so thick it can be felt." Exodus 10:4-5, 21

Chpt 11: Preparation for Passover

Moses said, "Thus says the Lord: 'About midnight I will go throughout Egypt, and all the firstborn in the land of Egypt will die, from the firstborn son of Pharaoh who sits on his throne, to the firstborn son of the slave girl who is at her hand mill, and all the firstborn of the cattle.
Exodus 11:4-5

Chpt 12: Passover and Deliverance

"This month is to be your beginning of months; it will be your first month of the year. Tell the whole community of Israel, 'In the tenth day of this month they each must take a lamb for themselves according to their families – a lamb for each household. If any household is too smal for a lamb, the man and his next-door neighbor are to take a lamb according to the number of people – you will make your count for the lamb according to how much each one can eat. Your lamb must be perfect, a male, one year old; you may take it from the sheep or from the goats.
Exodus 12:2-5

Exodus: The Birth of a Nation

Chpt 13: The Law of the Firstborn

The Lord spoke to Moses: "Set apart to me every firstborn male – the first offspring of every womb among the Israelites, whether human or animal; it is mine."

Moses took the bones of Joseph with him, for Joseph had made the Israelites solemnly swear...

Now the Lord was going before them by day in a pillar of cloud to lead them in the way, and by night in a pillar of fire to give them light, so that they could travel day or night.
Exodus 13:1-2, 19, 21

Chpt 14: Victory at the Red Sea

The Lord said to Moses, "Why do you cry out to me? Tell the Israelites to move on. And as for you, lift up your staff and extend your hand toward the sea and divide it, so that the Israelites may go through the middle of the sea on dry ground. And as for me, I am going to harden the hearts of the Egyptians so that they will come after them, that I may be honored because of Pharaoh and his army and his chariots and his horsemen. And the Egyptians will know that I am the Lord when I have gained my honor because of Pharaoh, his chariots, and his horsemen." Exodus 14:15-18

Chpt 15: Song of Triumph/Bitter Water

Then Moses and the Israelites sang this song to the Lord. They said, "I will sing to the Lord, for he has triumphed gloriously, the horse and its rider he has thrown into the sea.

Then Moses led Israel to journey away from the Red Sea. They went out to the Desert of Shur, walked for three days into the desert, and found no water. Then they came to Marah, but they were not able to drink the waters of Marah, because they were bitter. (That is why its name was Marah.)
Exodus 15:1, 22-23

Chpt 16: Manna from Heaven

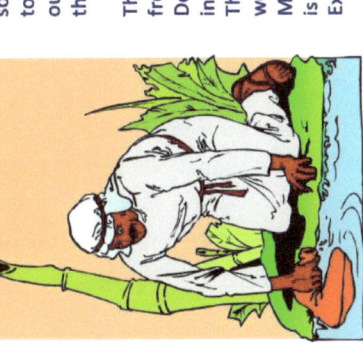

Then the Lord said to Moses, "I am going to rain bread from heaven for you, and the people will go out and gather the amount for each day, so that I may test them. Will they walk in my law or not? On the sixth day they will prepare what they bring in, and it will be twice as much as they gather every other day."
Exodus 16:4-5

Exodus: The Birth of a Nation

Chpt 17: Water from Rock & Amalekites

So the people contended with Moses, and they said, "Give us water to drink!" Moses said to them, "Why do you contend with me? Why do you test10 the Lord?"

The Lord said to Moses, "Write this as a memorial in the book, and rehearse it in Joshua's hearing; for I will surely wipe out the remembrance of Amalek from under heaven. Moses built an altar, and he called it "The Lord is my Banner," for he said, "For a hand was lifted up to the throne of the Lord – that the Lord will have war with Amalek from generation to generation." Exodus 17:2, 14-16

Chpt 18: Jethro's Advice to Moses

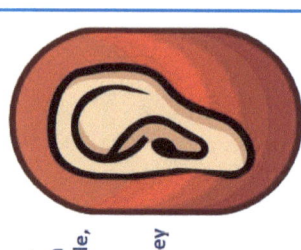

Moses listened to his father-in-law and did everything he had said. Moses chose capable men from all Israel, and he made them heads over the people, rulers of thousands, rulers of hundreds, rulers of fifties, and rulers of tens. They judged the people under normal circumstances; the difficult cases they would bring to Moses, but every small case they would judge themselves.

Exodus 18:24-26

Chpt 19: Israel at Mt. Sinai

In the third month after the Israelites went out from the land of Egypt, on the very day, they came to the Desert of Sinai. After they journeyed from Rephidim, they came to the Desert of Sinai, and they camped in the desert; Israel camped there in front of the mountain.
Exodus 19:1-2

Chpt 20: The Ten Commandments

God spoke all these words: "I, the Lord, am your God, who brought you from the land of Egypt, from the house of slavery. "You shall have no other gods before me.

Exodus 20:1-3

Exodus: The Birth of a Nation

Chpt 21: Personal Injury, Animals

"Whoever strikes someone so that he dies must surely be put to death. But if he does not do it with premeditation, but it happens by accident, then I will appoint for you a place where he may flee. But if a man willfully attacks his neighbor to kill him cunningly, you will take him even from my altar that he may die.

"If an ox gores a man or a woman so that either dies, then the ox must surely be stoned and its flesh must not be eaten, but the owner of the ox will be acquitted. Exodus 21:12-14, 28

Chpt 22: Property, Moral & Ceremony

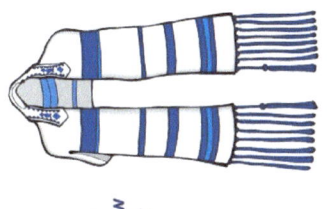

A thief must surely make full restitution; if he has nothing, then he will be sold for his theft.

"If a man seduces a virgin who is not engaged and has sexual relations with her, he must surely endow her to be his wife. If her father refuses to give her to him, he must pay money for the bride price of virgins.

"You will be holy people to me; you must not eat any meat torn by animals in the field. You must throw it to the dogs. Exodus 22:3, 16, 31

Chpt 23: Justice, Sabbath & Feasts

"You must not turn away justice for your poor people in their lawsuits. Keep your distance from a false charge – do not kill the innocent and the righteous, for I will not justify the wicked.

"You are also to observe the Feast of Harvest, the firstfruits of your labors that you have sown in the field, and the Feast of Ingathering at the end of the year when you have gathered in your harvest out of the field. At three times in the year all your males will appear before the Lord God.
Exodus 23:6-7, 16-17

Chpt 24: Lord Ratifies Covenant

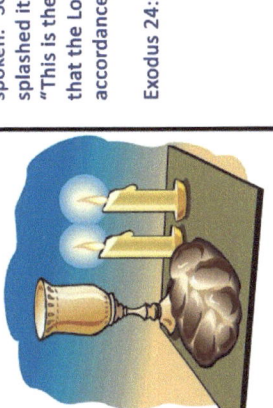

Moses took half of the blood and put it in bowls, and half of the blood he splashed on the altar. He took the Book of the Covenant and read it aloud to the people, and they said, "We are willing to do and obey all that the Lord has spoken." So Moses took the blood and splashed it on the people and said, "This is the blood of the covenant that the Lord has made with you in accordance with all these words."

Exodus 24:6-9

Exodus: The Birth of a Nation

Chpt 25: Ark of the Covenant

They are to make an ark of acacia wood – its length is to be three feet nine inches, its width two feet three inches, and its height two feet three inches.

I will meet with you there, and from above the atonement lid, from between the two cherubim that are over the ark of the testimony, I will speak with you about all that I will command you for the Israelites.
Exodus 25:10, 22

Chpt 26: The Tabernacle

The tabernacle itself you are to make with ten curtains of fine twisted linen and blue and purple and scarlet; you are to make them with cherubim that are the work of an artistic designer.
Exodus 26:1

Chpt 27: The Altar, Courtyard & Oil

"You are to make the altar of acacia wood, seven feet six inches long, and seven feet six inches wide; the altar is to be square, and its height is to be four feet six inches. You are to make its four horns on its four corners; its horns will be part of it, and you are to overlay it with bronze.
Exodus 27:1-2

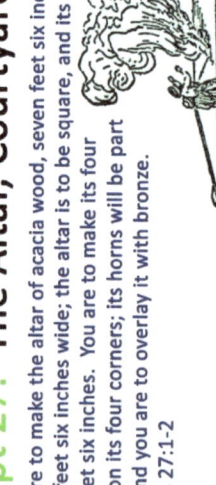

Chpt 28: Priest's Clothing

"They are to make the ephod of gold, blue, purple, scarlet, and fine twisted linen, the work of an artistic designer. It is to have two shoulder pieces attached to two of its corners, so it can be joined together. The artistically woven waistband of the ephod that is on it is to be like it, of one piece with the ephod, of gold, blue, purple, scarlet, and fine twisted linen

Exodus 28:6-9

Exodus: The Birth of a Nation

Chpt 29: Consecration of Aaron and Sons

"Now this is what you are to do for them to consecrate them so that they may minister as my priests. Take a young bull and two rams without blemish; and bread made without yeast, and perforated cakes without yeast mixed with oil, and wafers without yeast spread with oil – you are to make them using fine wheat flour. You are to put them in one basket and present them in the basket, along with the bull and the two rams.
Exodus 29:1-3

Chpt 30: Altar of Incense, Bronze Laver, Ransom Money, Oil & Incense

The Lord spoke to Moses: "You are also to make a large bronze basin with a bronze stand for washing. You are to put it between the tent of meeting and the altar and put water in it, and Aaron and his sons must wash their hands and their feet from it.

You are to make this into a sacred anointing oil, a perfumed compound, the work of a perfumer. It will be sacred anointing oil.
Exodus 30:17-19, 25

Chpt 31: Craftsmen

"See, I have chosen Bezalel son of Uri, the son of Hur, of the tribe of Judah, and I have filled him with the Spirit of God in skill, in understanding, in knowledge, and in all kinds of craftsmanship, to make artistic designs for work with gold, with silver, and with bronze, and with cutting and setting stone, and with cutting wood, to work in all kinds of craftsmanship.
Exodus 31:2-5

Chpt 32: Sin of the Golden Calf

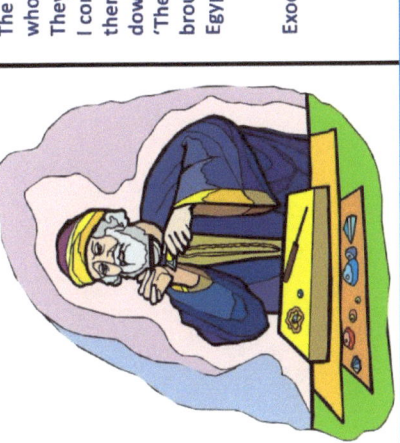

The Lord spoke to Moses: "Go quickly, descend, because your people, whom you brought up from the land of Egypt, have acted corruptly. They have quickly turned aside from the way that I commanded them – they have made for themselves a molten calf and have bowed down to it and sacrificed to it and said, 'These are your gods, O Israel, which brought you up from the land of Egypt.'"

Exodus 32:7-8

Exodus: The Birth of a Nation

Chpt 33: The Lord is Present

And whenever Moses entered the tent, the pillar of cloud would descend and stand at the entrance of the tent, and the Lord would speak with Moses. When all the people would see the pillar of cloud standing at the entrance of the tent, all the people, each one at the entrance of his own tent, would rise and worship. The Lord would speak to Moses face to face, the way a person speaks to a friend. Exodus 33:9-12

Chpt 34: New Ten Commandments

The Lord said to Moses, "Cut out two tablets of stone like the first, and I will write on the tablets the words that were on the first tablets, which you smashed. Be prepared in the morning, and go up in the morning to Mount Sinai, and station yourself for me there on the top of the mountain. No one is to come up with you; do not let anyone be seen anywhere on the mountain; not even the flocks or the herds may graze in front of that mountain." So Moses cut out two tablets of stone like the first; early in the morning he went up to Mount Sinai, just as the Lord had commanded him, and he took in his hand the two tablets of stone. Exodus 34:1-4

Chpt 35: Sabbath Rest

Moses assembled the whole community of the Israelites and said to them, "These are the things that the Lord has commanded you to do. In six days work may be done, but on the seventh day there must be a holy day for you, a Sabbath of complete rest to the Lord. Anyone who does work on it will be put to death. You must not kindle a fire in any of your homes on the Sabbath day." Exodus 35:1-3

Chpt 36: Building of the Tabernacle

All the skilled among those who were doing the work made the tabernacle with ten curtains of fine twisted linen and blue and purple and scarlet; they were made with cherubim that were the work of an artistic designer. Exodus 36:8

Exodus: The Birth of a Nation

Chpt 37: Objects for Tabernacle

Bezalel made the ark of acacia wood; its length was three feet nine inches, its width two feet three inches, and its height two feet three inches…He made the table of acacia wood; its length was three feet, its width one foot six inches, and its height two feet three inches…He made the lampstand of pure gold…He made the incense altar of acacia wood.
Exodus 37:1, 10, 17, 25

Chpt 38: The Courtyard

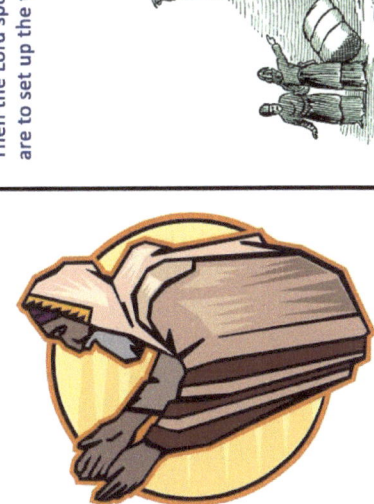

He made the courtyard. For the south side4 the hangings of the courtyard were of fine twisted linen, one hundred fifty feet long, with their twenty posts and their twenty bronze bases, with the hooks of the posts and their bands of silver. For the north side the hangings were one hundred fifty feet, with their twenty posts and their twenty bronze bases, with the hooks of the posts and their bands of silver.
Exodus 38:9-12

Chpt 39: Creating the Priestly Garments

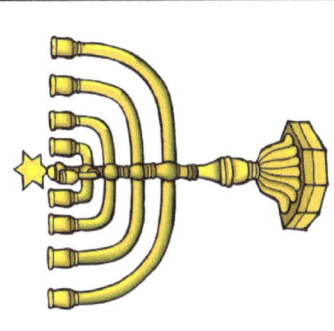

From the blue, purple, and scarlet yarn they made woven garments for serving in the sanctuary; they made holy garments that were for Aaron, just as the Lord had commanded Moses.
Exodus 39:1

Chpt 40: Setting Up the Sanctuary

Then the Lord spoke to Moses: "On the first day of the first month you are to set up the tabernacle, the tent of meeting. Exodus 40:1-2

Section 3

Leviticus: The Law of a Nation

Chpt 1: Sacrificial Regulations

Then the Lord called to Moses and spoke to him from the Meeting Tent: "Speak to the Israelites and tell them, 'When someone among you presents an offering to the Lord, you must present your offering from the domesticated animals, either from the herd or from the flock.
Leviticus 1:1-2

Chpt 2: Grain Offerings

"When a person presents a grain offering to the Lord, his offering must consist of choice wheat flour, and he must pour olive oil on it and put frankincense on it. Then he must bring it to the sons of Aaron, the priests, and the priest must scoop out from there a handful of its choice wheat flour and some of its olive oil in addition to all of its frankincense, and the priest must offer its memorial portion up in smoke on the altar – it is a gift of a soothing aroma to the Lord. The remainder of the grain offering belongs to Aaron and to his sons – it is most holy from the gifts of the Lord. Leviticus 2:1-3

Chpt 3: Peace Offerings

"Now if his offering is a peace offering sacrifice, if he presents an offering from the herd, he must present before the Lord a flawless male or a female. He must lay his hand on the head of his offering and slaughter it at the entrance of the Meeting Tent, and the sons of Aaron, the priests, must splash the blood against the altar's sides.
Leviticus 3:1-2

Chpt 4: Sin Offering Regulations

Then the Lord spoke to Moses: "Tell the Israelites, 'When a person sins by straying unintentionally from any of the Lord's commandments which must not be violated, and violates any one of them –
"'If the high priest sins so that the people are guilty, on account of the sin he has committed he must present a flawless young bull to the Lord for a sin offering.
Leviticus 4:1-4

Leviticus: The Law of a Nation

Chpt 5: Additional Sin Offerings

"When a person sins in that he hears a public curse against one who fails to testify and he is a witness (he either saw or knew what had happened) and he does not make it known, then he will bear his punishment for iniquity.
Leviticus 5:1

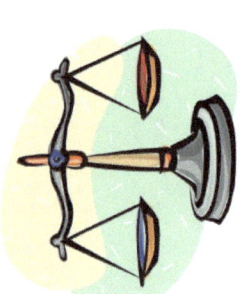

Chpt 6: Burnt Offering

Then the Lord spoke to Moses: "Command Aaron and his sons, 'This is the law of the burnt offering. The burnt offering is to remain on the hearth on the altar all night until morning, and the fire of the altar must be kept burning on it.
Leviticus 6:8-9

Chpt 7: Guilt Offering

"This is the law of the guilt offering. It is most holy. In the place where they slaughter the burnt offering they must slaughter the guilt offering, and the officiating priest must splash the blood against the altar's sides.
Leviticus 7:1-2

Chpt 8: Ordination of Priests

Then the Lord spoke to Moses: "Take Aaron and his sons with him, and the garments, the anointing oil, the sin offering bull, the two rams, and the basket of unleavened bread and assemble the whole congregation at the entrance of the Meeting Tent.
Leviticus 8:1-3

Leviticus: The Law of a Nation

Chpt 9: Preparing to Worship

On the eighth day Moses summoned Aaron and his sons and the elders of Israel, and said to Aaron, "Take for yourself a bull calf for a sin offering and a ram for a burnt offering, both flawless, and present them before the Lord. Then tell the Israelites: 'Take a male goat for a sin offering and a calf and lamb, both a year old and flawless, for a burnt offering, and an ox and a ram for peace offerings to sacrifice before the Lord, and a grain offering mixed with olive oil, for today the Lord is going to appear to you.'"
Leviticus 9:1-4

Chpt 10: Nadab and Abihu

Then Aaron's sons, Nadab and Abihu, each took his fire pan and put fire in it, set incense on it, and presented strange fire before the Lord, which he had not commanded them to do. So fire went out from the presence of the Lord and consumed them so that they died before the Lord. Leviticus 10:1-2

Chpt 11: Clean and Unclean Creatures

The Lord spoke to Moses and Aaron, saying to them, "Tell the Israelites: 'This is the kind of creature you may eat from among all the animals that are on the land. You may eat any among the animals that has a divided hoof (the hooves are completely split in two) and that also chews the cud. However, you must not eat these from among those that chew the cud and have divided hooves: The camel is unclean to you because it chews the cud even though its hoof is not divided.
Leviticus 11:1-3

Chpt 12: Women After Childbirth

The Lord spoke to Moses: "Tell the Israelites, 'When a woman produces offspring1 and bears a male child, she will be unclean seven days, as she is unclean during the days of her menstruation. On the eighth day the flesh of his foreskin must be circumcised. Then she will remain thirty-three days in blood purity.
Leviticus 12:1-4a

Leviticus: The Law of a Nation

Chpt 13: Dealing with Skin Problems

The Lord spoke to Moses and Aaron: "When someone has a swelling or a scab or a bright spot on the skin of his body that may become a diseased infection, he must be brought to Aaron the priest or one of his sons, the priests. The priest must then examine the infection on the skin of the body, and if the hair in the infection has turned white and the infection appears to be deeper than the skin of the body, so when the priest examines it he must pronounce the person unclean.
Leviticus 13:1-3

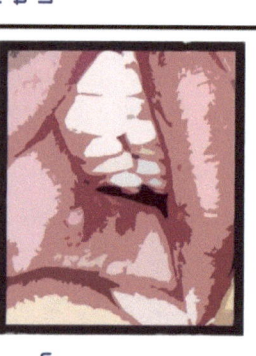

Chpt 14: Skin Disease Purification

The Lord spoke to Moses: "This is the law of the diseased person on the day of his purification, when he is brought to the priest.
Leviticus 14:1

Chpt 15: Bodily Discharges

The Lord spoke to Moses and Aaron: "Speak to the Israelites and tell them, 'When any man has a discharge from his body, his discharge is unclean...' "Thus you are to set the Israelites apart from their impurity so that they do not die in their impurity by defiling my tabernacle which is in their midst.
Leviticus 15:1, 31

Chpt 16: Day of Atonement

"This is to be a perpetual statute for you. In the seventh month, on the tenth day of the month, you must humble yourselves and do no work of any kind, both the native citizen and the foreigner who resides in your midst, for on this day atonement is to be made for you to cleanse you from all your sins; you must be clean before the Lord. It is to be a Sabbath of complete rest for you, and you must humble yourselves. It is a perpetual statute.
Leviticus 16:29-31

Leviticus: The Law of a Nation

Chpt 17: Dealing with Animals

The Lord spoke to Moses: "Speak to Aaron, his sons, and all the Israelites, and tell them: 'This is the word that the Lord has commanded: "Blood guilt will be accounted to any man from the house of Israel who slaughters an ox or a lamb or a goat inside the camp or outside the camp, but has not brought it to the entrance of the Meeting Tent to present it as6 an offering to the Lord before the tabernacle of the Lord.
Leviticus 17:1-4

Chpt 18: Obedience in All of Life

The Lord spoke to Moses: "Speak to the Israelites and tell them, 'I am the Lord your God! You must not do as they do in the land of Egypt where you have been living, and you must not do as they do in the land of Canaan into which I am about to bring you; you must not walk in their statutes. You must observe my regulations and you must be sure to walk in my statutes. I am the Lord your God. So you must keep my statutes and my regulations; anyone who does so will live by keeping them. I am the Lord.
Leviticus 18:1-5

Chpt 19: Religious & Social Regulations

The Lord spoke to Moses: "Speak to the whole congregation of the Israelites and tell them, 'You must be holy because I, the Lord your God, am holy. Each of you must respect his mother and his father, and you must keep my Sabbaths. I am the Lord your God. Do not turn to idols, and you must not make for yourselves gods of cast metal. I am the Lord your God.
Leviticus 19:1-4

Chpt 20: Holy Rules for Families

The Lord spoke to Moses: "You are to say to the Israelites, 'Any man from the Israelites or from the foreigners who reside in Israel who gives any of his children to Molech must be put to death; the people of the land must pelt him with stones. I myself will set my face against that man and cut him off from the midst of his people, because he has given some of his children to Molech and thereby defiled my sanctuary and profaned my holy name.
Leviticus 20:1-3

Leviticus: The Law of a Nation

Chpt 21: Rules for Priests

The Lord said to Moses: "Say to the priests, the sons of Aaron – say to them, 'For a dead person no priest is to defile himself among his people, except for his close relative who is near to him: his mother, his father, his son, his daughter, his brother, and his virgin sister who is near to him, who has no husband; he may defile himself for her.
Leviticus 21:1-3

Chpt 22: Stipends, Votive, Freewill

"No lay person may eat anything holy. Neither a priest's lodger nor a hired laborer may eat anything holy, but if a priest buys a person with his own money, that person may eat the holy offerings, and those born in the priest's own house may eat his food.
Leviticus 22:10-11

Chpt 23: Festivals and First Fruits

The Lord spoke to Moses: "Speak to the Israelites and tell them, 'These are the Lord's appointed times which you must proclaim as holy assemblies — my appointed times: "'Six days work may be done, but on the seventh day there must be a Sabbath of complete rest, a holy assembly. You must not do any work; it is a Sabbath to the Lord in all the places where you live.
Leviticus 23:1-4

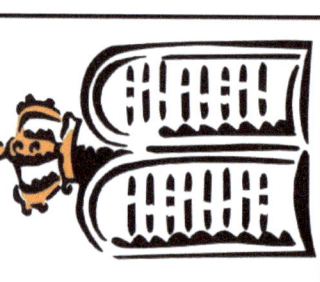

Chpt 24: Blaspheming God's Name

Then the Lord spoke to Moses: "Bring the one who cursed outside the camp, and all who heard him are to lay their hands on his head, and the whole congregation is to stone him to death. Moreover, you are to tell the Israelites, 'If any man curses his God he will bear responsibility for his sin, and one who misuses the name of the Lord must surely be put to death.
Leviticus 24:13-14

Leviticus: The Law of a Nation

Chpt 25: Rules for Sabbath Year, Etc.

The Lord spoke to Moses at Mount Sinai: "Speak to the Israelites and tell them, 'When you enter the land that I am giving you, the land must observe a Sabbath1 to the Lord. Six years you may sow your field, and six years you may prune your vineyard and gather the produce, but in the seventh year the land must have a Sabbath of complete rest – a Sabbath to the Lord. You must not sow your field or prune your vineyard. Leviticus 25:1-4

Chpt 26: Obey, Confess, Repent

"'If you walk in my statutes and are sure to obey my commandments, I will give you your rains in their time so that the land will give its yield and the trees of the field will produce their fruit. Threshing season will extend for you until the season for harvesting grapes, and the season for harvesting grapes will extend until sowing season, so you will eat your bread until you are satisfied, and you will live securely in your land. I will grant peace in the land so that you will lie down to sleep without anyone terrifying you. I will remove harmful animals from the land, and no sword of war will pass through your land. Leviticus 26:3-6

Chpt 27: Regulations for Redemption

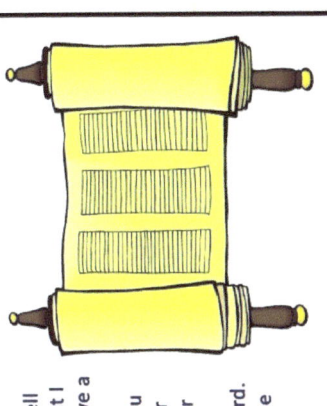

The Lord spoke to Moses: "Speak to the Israelites and tell them, 'When a man makes a special votive offering based on the conversion value of persons to the Lord, Leviticus 27:1-2

~ End of Leviticus ~

Section 4

Numbers: Wilderness Wanderings

Chpt 1: The Census of the Tribes

So Moses and Aaron took these men who had been mentioned specifically by name, and they assembled the entire community together on the first day of the second month. Then the people recorded their ancestry by their clans and families, and the men who were twenty years old or older were listed by name individually, just as the Lord had commanded Moses. And so he numbered them in the wilderness of Sinai. Numbers 1:17-19

Chpt 2: Arranging the Tribes

The Lord spoke to Moses and to Aaron: "Every one of the Israelites must camp under his standard with the emblems of his family; they must camp at some distance around the tent of meeting."
Numbers 2:1

Chpt 3: Numbering of Levites

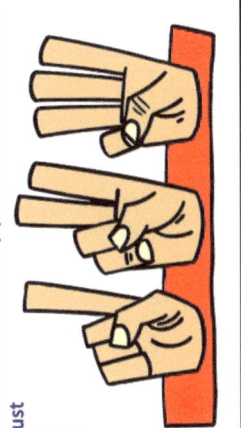

Then the Lord spoke to Moses in the wilderness of Sinai: "Number the Levites by their clans and their families; every male from a month old and upward you are to number." So Moses numbered them according to the word of the Lord, just as he had been commanded.
Numbers 3:14-16

Chpt 4: Those Called to Service

Then the Lord spoke to Moses and Aaron: "Take a census of the Kohathites from among the Levites, by their families and by their clans, from thirty years old and upward to fifty years old, all who enter the company to do the work in the tent of meeting. This is the service of the Kohathites in the tent of meeting, relating to the most holy things."
Numbers 4:1-4

Numbers: Wilderness Wanderings

Chpt 5: Unclean, Restitution, Jealousy

Then the Lord spoke to Moses: "Command the Israelites to expel from the camp every leper, everyone who has a discharge, and whoever becomes defiled by a corpse...Then the Lord spoke to Moses: "Tell the Israelites, 'When a man or a woman commits any sin that people commit, thereby breaking faith with the Lord...The Lord spoke to Moses: "Speak to the Israelites and tell them, 'If any man's wife goes astray and behaves unfaithfully toward him, and a man has sexual relations with her without her husband knowing it'..."
Numbers 5:1-2, 5-7, 11-13a

Chpt 6: Nazarite and Other Vows

Then the Lord spoke to Moses: "Speak to the Israelites, and tell them, 'When either a man or a woman takes a special vow, to take a vow as a Nazirite, to separate himself to the Lord, he must separate himself from wine and strong drink, he must drink neither vinegar made from wine nor vinegar made from strong drink, nor may he drink any juice of grapes, nor eat fresh grapes or raisins. All the days of his separation he must not eat anything that is produced by the grapevine, from seed to skin'."
Numbers 6:1-4

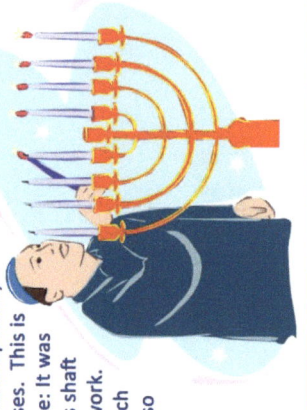

Chpt 7: Offerings and Gifts

Then the Lord spoke to Moses: "Receive these gifts from them, that they may be used in doing the work of the tent of meeting; and you must give them to the Levites, to every man as his service requires."
Numbers 7:4-6

Chpt 8: The Lamps and the Levites

The Lord spoke to Moses: "Speak to Aaron and tell him, 'When you set up the lamps, the seven lamps are to give light in front of the lampstand.'" And Aaron did so; he set up the lamps to face toward the front of the lampstand, as the Lord commanded Moses. This is how the lampstand was made: It was beaten work in gold; from its shaft to its flowers it was beaten work. According to the pattern which the Lord had shown Moses, so he made the lampstand.
Numbers 8:1-4

Numbers: Wilderness Wanderings

Chpt 9: Passover Regulations

The Lord spoke to Moses in the wilderness of Sinai, in the first month of the second year after they had come out of the land of Egypt: "The Israelites are to observe the Passover at its appointed time. In the fourteenth day of this month, at twilight, you are to observe it at its appointed time; you must keep it in accordance with all its statutes and all its customs." Numbers 9:1-3

Chpt 10: Blowing of the Trumpets

The Lord spoke to Moses: "Make two trumpets of silver; you are to make them from a single hammered piece. You will use them for assembling the community and for directing the traveling of the camps. When they blow them both, all the community must come to you to the entrance of the tent of meeting." Numbers 10:1-3

Chpt 11: Israelites Complain

When the people complained, it displeased the Lord. When the Lord heard it, his anger burned, and so the fire of the Lord burned among them and consumed some of the outer parts of the camp. Numbers 11:1

Chpt 12: Those Against Moses

Then Miriam and Aaron spoke against Moses because of the Cushite woman he had married (for he had married an Ethiopian woman). They said, "Has the Lord only spoken through Moses? Has he not also spoken through us?" And the Lord heard it. (Now the man Moses was very humble, more so than any man on the face of the earth.) Numbers 12:1-3

Numbers: Wilderness Wanderings

Chpt 13: Spies are Sent to Canaan

The Lord spoke to Moses: "Send out men to investigate the land of Canaan, which I am giving to the Israelites. You are to send one man from each ancestral tribe, each one a leader among them." So Moses sent them from the wilderness of Paran at the command of the Lord. All of them were leaders of the Israelites. Numbers 13:1-3

Chpt 14: Israel's Unbelief and Anger

Then all the community raised a loud cry, and the people wept that night. And all the Israelites murmured against Moses and Aaron, and the whole congregation said to them, "If only we had died in the land of Egypt, or if only we had perished6 in this wilderness! Why has the Lord brought us into this land only to be killed by the sword, that our wives and our children should become plunder? Wouldn't it be better for us to return to Egypt?" So they said to one another, "Let's appoint a leader and return to Egypt." Numbers 14:1-4

Chpt 15: Firstfruits, Tassels, Etc.

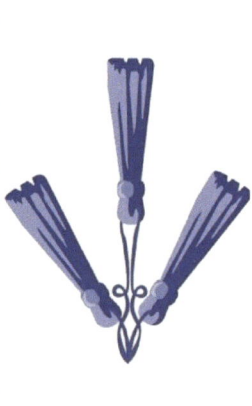

The Lord spoke to Moses: "Speak to the Israelites and tell them, 'When you enter the land where you are to live, which I am giving you, and you make an offering by fire to the Lord from the herd or from the flock (whether a burnt offering or a sacrifice for discharging a vow or as a freewill offering or in your solemn feasts) to create a pleasing aroma to the Lord, Numbers 15:1-3

Chpt 16: Rebellion of Korah

Korah son of Izhar, the son of Kohath, the son of Levi, and Dathan and Abiram, the sons of Eliab, and On son of Peleth, who were Reubenites, took men and rebelled against Moses, along with some of the Israelites, leaders of the community, chosen from the assembly, famous men. And they assembled against Moses and Aaron, saying to them, "You take too much upon yourselves, seeing that the whole community is holy, every one of them, and the Lord is among them. Why then do you exalt yourselves above the community of the Lord?" Numbers 16:1-3

Numbers: Wilderness Wanderings

Chpt 17: Budding of Aaron's Staff

The Lord spoke to Moses: "Speak to the Israelites, and receive from them a staff from each tribe, one from every tribal leader, twelve staffs; you must write each man's name on his staff. You must write Aaron's name on the staff of Levi; for one staff is for the head of every tribe. You must place them in the tent of meeting before the ark of the covenant where I meet with you. And the staff of the man whom I choose will blossom; so I will rid myself of the complaints of the Israelites, which they murmur against you." Numbers 17:1-5

Chpt 18: Duties and Portion of Priests

The Lord said to Aaron, "You and your sons and your tribe with you must bear the iniquity of the sanctuary, and you and your sons with you must bear the iniquity of your priesthood."
Numbers 18:1

Chpt 19: Red Heiffer

The Lord spoke to Moses and Aaron: "This is the ordinance of the law which the Lord has commanded: 'Instruct the Israelites to bring you a red heifer without blemish, which has no defect and has never carried a yoke. You must give it to Eleazar the priest so that he can take it outside the camp, and it must be slaughtered before him. Eleazar the priest is to take some of its blood with his finger, and sprinkle some of the blood seven times directly in front of the tent of meeting.'" Numbers 19:1-4

Chpt 20: Israelites Complain…Again

Then the entire community of Israel entered the wilderness of Zin in the first month, and the people stayed in Kadesh. Miriam died and was buried there. And there was no water for the community, and so they gathered themselves together against Moses and Aaron. The people contended with Moses, saying, "If only we had died when our brothers died before the Lord!" Numbers 20:1-3

Numbers: Wilderness Wanderings

Chpt 21: Fiery Serpents

Then they traveled from Mount Hor by the road to the Red Sea, to go around the land of Edom, but the people became impatient along the way. And the people spoke against God and against Moses, "Why have you brought us up out of Egypt to die in the wilderness, for there is no bread or water, and we detest this worthless food." So the Lord sent poisonous snakes among the people, and they bit the people; many people of Israel died. Then the people came to Moses and said, "We have sinned, for we have spoken against the Lord and against you. Pray to the Lord that he would take away the snakes from us." Numbers 21:1-7a

Chpt 22: God Opposes Balaam

So Balaam got up in the morning, and said to the princes of Balak, "Go to your land, for the Lord has refused to permit me to go with you." So the princes of Moab departed and went back to Balak and said, "Balaam refused to come with us."
Numbers 22:13-14

Chpt 23: Balaam Blesses Israel

Balaam said to Balak, "Build me seven altars here, and prepare for me here seven bulls and seven rams." So Balak did just as Balaam had said. Balak and Balaam then offered on each altar a bull and a ram. Balaam said to Balak, "Station yourself by your burnt offering, and I will go off; perhaps the Lord will come to meet me, and whatever he reveals to me I will tell you." Then he went to a deserted height. Numbers 23:1-3

Chpt 24: Balaam Prophesies

When Balaam saw that it pleased the Lord to bless Israel, he did not go as at the other times to seek for omens, but he set his face toward the wilderness. When Balaam lifted up his eyes, he saw Israel camped tribe by tribe; and the Spirit of God came upon him.
Numbers 24:1-2

Numbers: Wilderness Wanderings

Chpt 25: Sexual Immorality & Baal

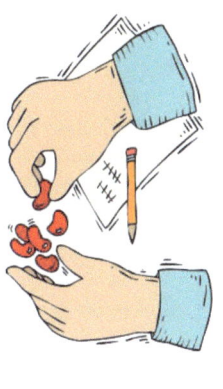

When Israel lived in Shittim, the people began to commit sexual immorality with the daughters of Moab. These women invited the people to the sacrifices of their gods; then the people ate and bowed down to their gods. When Israel joined themselves to Baal-peor, the anger of the Lord flared up against Israel. Numbers 25:1-3

Chpt 26: A Second Census

After the plague the Lord said to Moses and to Eleazar son of Aaron the priest, "Take a census of the whole community of Israelites, from twenty years old and upward, by their clans, everyone who can serve in the army of Israel." Numbers 26:1-2

Chpt 27: Leadership Changes

Then the Lord said to Moses, "Go up this mountain of the Abarim range, and see the land I have given to the Israelites. When you have seen it, you will be gathered to your ancestors, as Aaron your brother was gathered to his ancestors. For in the wilderness of Zin when the community rebelled against me, you rebelled against my command to show me as holy before their eyes over the water – the water of Meribah in Kadesh in the wilderness of Zin." Numbers 27:12-14

Chpt 28: Offerings; Sweet Aroma

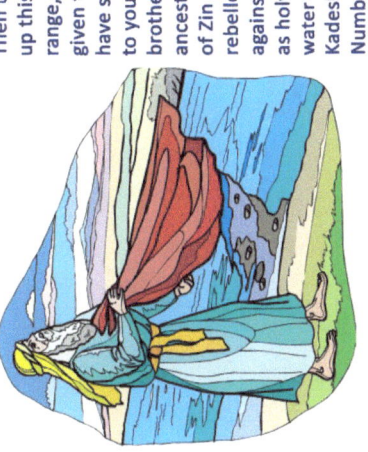

The Lord spoke to Moses: "Command the Israelites: 'With regard to my offering, be sure to offer my food for my offering made by fire, as a pleasing aroma to me at its appointed time.'" Numbers 28:1-2

Numbers: Wilderness Wanderings

Chpt 29: Feast of Shelters; Atonement

"On the first day of the seventh month, you are to hold a holy assembly. You must not do your ordinary work, for it is a day of blowing trumpets for you...On the tenth day of this seventh month you are to have a holy assembly. You must humble yourselves; you must not do any work on it...On the fifteenth day of the seventh month you are to have a holy assembly; you must do no ordinary work, and you must keep a festival to the Lord for seven days." Numbers 29:1, 7, 12

Chpt 30: Making Vows

Moses told the leaders of the tribes concerning the Israelites, "This is what the Lord has commanded: If a man makes a vow to the Lord or takes an oath of binding obligation on himself, he must not break his word, but must do whatever he has promised." Numbers 30:1-2

Chpt 31: Battle with the Midianites

The Lord spoke to Moses: "Exact vengeance for the Israelites on the Midianites – after that you will be gathered to your people." So Moses spoke to the people: "Arm men from among you for the war, to attack the Midianites and to execute the Lord's vengeance on Midian. You must send to the battle a thousand men from every tribe throughout all the tribes of Israel." Numbers 31:1-4

Chpt 32: Request by the Reubenites

Now the Reubenites and the Gadites possessed a very large number of cattle. When they saw that the lands of Jazer and Gilead were ideal for cattle, the Gadites and the Reubenites came and addressed Moses, Eleazar the priest, and the leaders of the community. Numbers 32:1-2

Numbers: Wilderness Wanderings

Chpt 33: Journeys Recounted

These are the journeys of the Israelites, who went out of the land of Egypt by their divisions under the authority of Moses and Aaron. Moses recorded their departures according to their journeys, by the commandment of the Lord; now these are their journeys according to their departures.
Numbers 33:1-2

Chpt 34: At the Edge of Canaan

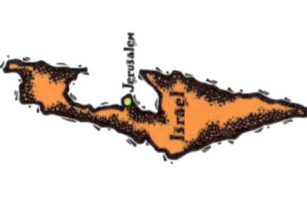

Then the Lord spoke to Moses: "Give these instructions to the Israelites, and tell them: 'When you enter Canaan, the land that has been assigned to you as an inheritance, the land of Canaan with its borders your southern border will extend from the wilderness of Zin along the Edomite border, and your southern border will run eastward to the extremity of the Salt Sea, and then the border will turn from the south to the Scorpion Ascent, continue to Zin, and then its direction will be from the south to Kadesh Barnea. Then it will go to Hazar Addar and pass over to Azmon.'" Numbers 34:1-4

Chpt 35: Cities of Levites; Refuge

Then the Lord spoke to Moses in the Moabite plains by the Jordan near Jericho. He said: "Instruct the Israelites to give the Levites towns to live in from the inheritance the Israelites will possess..." Then the Lord spoke to Moses: "Speak to the Israelites and tell them, 'When you cross over the Jordan River into the land of Canaan, you must then designate some towns as towns of refuge for you, to which a person who has killed someone unintentionally may flee'." Numbers 35:1, 9-4

Chpt 36: Women & Land Inheritance

Then the heads of the family groups of the Gileadites, the descendant of Machir, the descendant of Manasseh, who were from the Josephite families, approached and spoke before Moses and the leaders who were the heads of the Israelite families. They said, "The Lord commanded my lord to give the land as an inheritance by lot to the Israelites; and my lord was commanded by the Lord to give the inheritance of our brother Zelophehad to his daughters." Numbers 36:1-2

Section 5

Deuteronomy: Review of the Law

Chpt 1: Reviewing Kadesh Barnea

You were not willing to go up, however, but instead rebelled against the Lord your God. You complained among yourselves privately and said, "Because the Lord hates us he brought us from Egypt to deliver us over to the Amorites so they could destroy us!
Deuteronomy 1:26-27

Chpt 2: From Kadesh Barnea to Moab

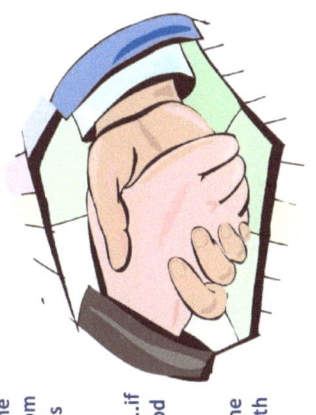

Then we turned and set out toward the desert land on the way to the Red Sea just as the Lord told me to do, detouring around Mount Seir for a long time. At this point the Lord said to me, "You have circled around this mountain long enough; now turn north. Instruct these people as follows: 'You are about to cross the border of your relatives the descendants of Esau, who inhabit Seir. They will be afraid of you, so watch yourselves carefully. Do not be hostile toward them, because I am not giving you any of their land, not even a footprint, for I have given Mount Seir as an inheritance for Esau.
Deuteronomy 2:1-5

Chpt 3: King Og's (Nephilim?) Defeat

Next we set out on the route to Bashan, but King Og of Bashan and his whole army came out to meet us in battle at Edrei. The Lord, however, said to me, "Don't be afraid of him because I have already given him, his whole army, and his land to you. You will do to him exactly what you did to King Sihon of the Amorites who lived in Heshbon."
Deuteronomy 3:1-2

Chpt 4: Covenants & God's Nature

Be very careful, then, because you saw no form at the time the Lord spoke to you at Horeb from the middle of the fire. I say this so you will not corrupt yourselves by making an image in the form of any kind of figure...if you return to the Lord your God and obey him (for he is a merciful God), he will not let you down or destroy you, for he cannot forget the covenant with your ancestors that he confirmed by oath to them.
Deuteronomy 4:15-16a, 30B

Deuteronomy: Review of the Law

Chpt 5: Ten Commandments

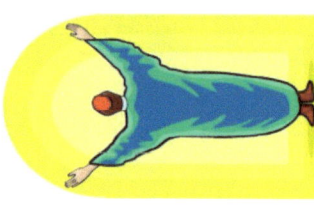

Then Moses called all the people of Israel together and said to them: "Listen, Israel, to the statutes and ordinances that I am about to deliver to you today; learn them and be careful to keep them..."
Deuteronomy 5:1

Chpt 6: Worship Only the Lord

You must revere the Lord your God, serve him, and take oaths using only his name. You must not go after other gods, those of the surrounding peoples, for the Lord your God, who is present among you, is a jealous God and his anger will erupt against you and remove you from the land
Deuteronomy 6:13-15

Chpt 7: The Reason Israel was Elected

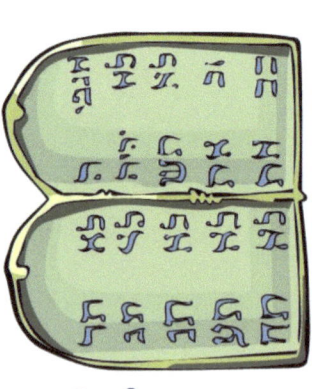

It is not because you were more numerous than all the other peoples that the Lord favored and chose you – for in fact you were the least numerous of all peoples. Rather it is because of his love for you and his faithfulness to the promise he solemnly vowed to your ancestors that the Lord brought you out with great power, redeeming you from the place of slavery, from the power of Pharaoh king of Egypt.
Deuteronomy 7:7-8

Chpt 8: The Lord Provided

You must keep carefully all these commandments I am giving you today so that you may live, increase in number, and go in and occupy the land that the Lord promised to your ancestors. Remember the whole way by which he has brought you these forty years through the desert so that he might, by humbling you, test you to see if you have it within you to keep his commandments or not.
Deuteronomy 8:1-2

Deuteronomy: Review of the Law

Chpt 9: Wickedness in Canaan

Do not think to yourself after the Lord your God has driven them out before you, "Because of my own righteousness the Lord has brought me here to possess this land." It is because of the wickedness of these nations that the Lord is driving them out ahead of you.
Deuteronomy 9:4

Chpt 10: More Ordinances & Laws

At that same time the Lord said to me, "Carve out for yourself two stone tablets like the first ones and come up the mountain to me; also make for yourself a wooden ark. I will write on the tablets the same words that were on the first tablets you broke, and you must put them into the ark."
Deuteronomy 10:1-2

Chpt 11: Abundance of Canaan

Now pay attention to all the commandments I am giving you today, so that you may be strong enough to enter and possess the land where you are headed, and that you may enjoy long life in the land the Lord promised to give to your ancestors and their descendants, a land flowing with milk and honey.
Deuteronomy 11:8-9

Chpt 12: The Sanctuary

When you do go across the Jordan River and settle in the land he is granting you as an inheritance and you find relief from all the enemies who surround you, you will live in safety. Then you must come to the place the Lord your God chooses for his name to reside, bringing everything I am commanding you – your burnt offerings, sacrifices, tithes, the personal offerings you have prepared, and all your choice votive offerings which you devote to him.
Deuteronomy 12:10-11

Deuteronomy: Review of the Law

Chpt 13: Idolatry and False Prophets

You must be careful to do everything I am commanding you. Do not add to it or subtract from it! Suppose a prophet or one who foretells by dreams should appear among you and show you a sign or wonder, and the sign or wonder should come to pass concerning what he said to you, namely, "Let us follow other gods" – gods whom you have not previously known – "and let us serve them."
Deuteronomy 13:1-2

Chpt 14: The Holy and Profane

You are children of the Lord your God. Do not cut yourselves or shave your forehead bald for the sake of the dead. For you are a people holy to the Lord your God. He has chosen you to be his people, prized above all others on the face of the earth.
Deuteronomy 14:1-2

Chpt 15: Regulations Related to Debt

At the end of every seven years you must declare a cancellation of debts. This is the nature of the cancellation: Every creditor must remit what he has loaned to another person; he must not force payment from his fellow Israelite, for it is to be recognized as "the Lord's cancellation of debts."
Deuteronomy 15:1-2

Chpt 16: Passover and Festivals

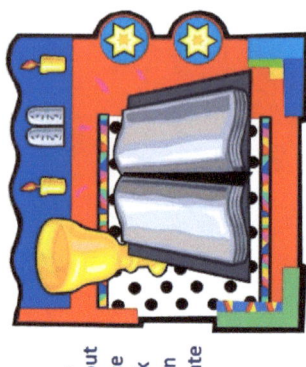

Observe the month Abib and keep the Passover to the Lord your God, for in that month he brought you out of Egypt by night. You must sacrifice the Passover animal (from the flock or the herd) to the Lord your God in the place where he chooses to locate his name.
Deuteronomy 16:1-2

Deuteronomy: Review of the Law

Chpt 17: Legal Situations and Kingship

If a matter is too difficult for you to judge – bloodshed, legal claim, or assault – matters of controversy in your villages – you must leave there and go up to the place the Lord your God chooses...When you come to the land the Lord your God is giving you and take it over and live in it and then say, "I will select a king like all the nations surrounding me," you must select without fail a king whom the Lord your God chooses.
Deuteronomy 17:8, 14-15a

Chpt 18: Provision for Priests/Levites

The Levitical priests1 – indeed, the entire tribe of Levi – will have no allotment or inheritance with Israel; they may eat the burnt offerings of the Lord and of his inheritance.
Deuteronomy 18:1

Chpt 19: Laws Related to Manslaughter

Now this is the law pertaining to one who flees there in order to live, if he has accidentally killed another without hating him at the time of the accident.
Deuteronomy 19:4

Chpt 20: Laws Dealing with War

When you go to war against your enemies and see chariotry and troops who outnumber you, do not be afraid of them, for the Lord your God, who brought you up out of the land of Egypt, is with you. As you move forward for battle, the priest will approach and say to the soldiers, "Listen, Israel! Today you are moving forward to do battle with your enemies. Do not be fainthearted. Do not fear and tremble or be terrified because of them, for the Lord your God goes with you to fight on your behalf against your enemies to give you victory."
Deuteronomy 20:1-4

Deuteronomy: Review of the Law

Chpt 21: Family Laws and Unsolved Murder

If a homicide victim should be found lying in a field in the land the Lord your God is giving you, and no one knows who killed him, your elders and judges must go out and measure how far it is to the cities in the vicinity of the corpse...If a person commits a sin punishable by death and is executed, and you hang the corpse on a tree, his body must not remain all night on the tree; instead you must make certain you bury him that same day, for the one who is left exposed on a tree is cursed by God. You must not defile your land which the Lord your God is giving you as an inheritance. Deuteronomy 21:1-2, 22-23

Chpt 22: Laws of Purity

You must not plant your vineyard with two kinds of seed; otherwise the entire yield, both of the seed you plant and the produce of the vineyard, will be defiled. You must not plow with an ox and a donkey harnessed together. You must not wear clothing made with wool and linen meshed together. You shall make yourselves tassels for the four corners of the clothing you wear. Deuteronomy 22:9-12

Chpt 23: More Laws on Purity

A man with crushed or severed genitals may not enter the assembly of the Lord. A person of illegitimate birth may not enter the assembly of the Lord; to the tenth generation no one related to him may do so. An Ammonite or Moabite may not enter the assembly of the Lord; to the tenth generation none of their descendants shall ever do so, for they did not meet you with food and water on the way as you came from Egypt, and furthermore, they hired Balaam son of Beor of Pethor in Aram Naharaim to curse you. Deuteronomy 23:1-4

Chpt 24: Marriage and Human Dignity

When a man is newly married, he need not go into the army nor be obligated in any way; he must be free to stay at home for a full year and bring joy to the wife he has married...When you make any kind of loan to your neighbor, you may not go into his house to claim what he is offering as security. You must stand outside and the person to whom you are making the loan will bring out to you what he is offering as security. If the person is poor you may not use what he gives you as security for a covering. Deuteronomy 24:5, 10-12

Deuteronomy: Review of the Law

Chpt 25: Controversies for Judges

If controversy arises between people, they should go to court for judgment. When the judges hear the case, they shall exonerate the innocent but condemn4 the guilty. Deuteronomy 25:1

Chpt 26: First Fruits and Tithe

When you enter the land that the Lord your God is giving you as an inheritance, and you occupy it and live in it, you must take the first of all the ground's produce you harvest from the land the Lord your God is giving you, place it in a basket, and go to the place where he chooses to locate his name. Deuteronomy 26:1-2

Chpt 27: Obey the Lord or Be Cursed

"The Levites will call out to every Israelite with a loud voice: 'Cursed is the one who makes a carved or metal image – something abhorrent to the Lord, the work of the craftsman – and sets it up in a secret place.' Then all the people will say, 'Amen!' Deuteronomy 27:14-15

Chpt 28: Blessings and Curses

"If you indeed obey the Lord your God and are careful to observe all his commandments I am giving you today, the Lord your God will elevate you above all the nations of the earth. All these blessings will come to you in abundance if you obey the Lord your God: Deuteronomy 28:1-2

Deuteronomy: Review of the Law

Chpt 29: Results of Disobedience

Beware that the heart of no man, woman, clan, or tribe among you turns away from the Lord our God today to pursue and serve the gods of those nations; beware that there is among you no root producing poisonous and bitter fruit.
Deuteronomy 29:18

Chpt 30: When Covenant is Reaffirmed

"When you have experienced all these things, both the blessings and the curses I have set before you, you will reflect upon them in all the nations where the Lord your God has banished you. Then if you and your descendants turn to the Lord your God and obey him with your whole mind and being just as I am commanding you today, the Lord your God will reverse your captivity and have pity on you.
Deuteronomy 30:1-3b

Chpt 31: From Moses to Joshua

Then Moses went and spoke these words to all Israel. He said to them, "Today I am a hundred and twenty years old. I am no longer able to get about, and the Lord has said to me, 'You will not cross the Jordan.'
Deuteronomy 31:1-2

Chpt 32: Song of Moses

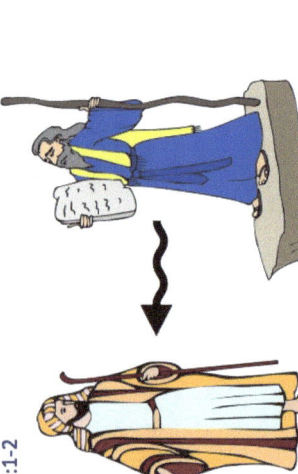

Listen, O heavens, and I will speak; hear, O earth, the words of my mouth. My teaching will drop like the rain, my sayings will drip like the dew, as rain drops upon the grass, and showers upon new growth. For I will proclaim the name of the Lord; you must acknowledge the greatness of our God.
Deuteronomy 32:1-3

Deuteronomy: Review of the Law

Chpt 33: Blessing of Moses on Israel

This is the blessing Moses the man of God pronounced upon the Israelites before his death. Deuteronomy 33:1

Chpt 34: Death of Moses

So Moses, the servant of the Lord, died there in the land of Moab as the Lord had said. He buried him in the land of Moab near Beth Peor, but no one knows his exact burial place to this very day. Moses was 120 years old when he died, but his eye was not dull nor had his vitality departed. The Israelites mourned for Moses in the deserts of Moab for thirty days; then the days of mourning for Moses ended. Deuteronomy 34:1-8

This is the end of *Genesis*, *Exodus*, *Leviticus*, *Numbers*, and *Deuteronomy*. We hope you have gained some valuable insight into the Pentateuch. Look for the remaining Old Testament books, as well as all the New Testament books, in pictorial outline format as well!

Stay tuned to our web pages for the most up to date information:
www.studygrowknow.com
www.studyknowgrow.com
www.rightly-dividing.com

STUDY • GROW • KNOW
It's always time to study, grow and know your faith!
www.studygrowknow.com

NOTES

Resources for Your Library:

BOOKS:

- A General Introduction to the Bible - Geisler & Nix
- An Historical Survey of the Old Testament - Eugene Merrill
- Archaeology and the Old Testament - Alfred Hoerth
- A New Translation of the Dead Sea Scrolls - Michael Wise
- Bible History: Old Testament - Alfred Edersheim
- Chronological Study Bible (NKJV) - Thomas Nelson Publishers
- Explore the Book – J. Sidlow Baxter
- The Everything Judaism Book – Richard Bank
- Footsteps of the Messiah - Arnold G. Fruchtenbaum
- For Zion's Sake: Christian Zionism and the Role of John Nelson Darby - Paul Richard Wilkinson
- God's Plan for Israel - Steven A. Kreloff
- Israel: A History - Martin Gilbert
- Israel in the Plan of God - David Baron
- Israelology: Missing Link in Systematic Theology - Arnold G. Fruchtenbaum
- Nelson's Old Testament Survey - Thomas Nelson Publishers
- The Temple: Its Ministry and Services - Alfred Edersheim
- The Temple and Bible Prophecy - Randall Price
- Unfolding Drama of Redemption - W. Graham Scroggie
- Unger's Commentary on the Old Testament - Merrill F. Unger

Order These Other Books by Fred DeRuvo

www.createspace.com • www.amazon.com • www.studygrowknow.com

The Anti-Supernatural Bias of Ex-Christians (and Other Important Topics)
Look into the testimonies of folks who refer to themselves as Ex-Christians. Are they, or are they kidding themselves? Fred goes back to the Bible to determine the truth of their words. Other topics deal with the Rapture, the Israelites as slaves in Egypt and more. 240 pages, $11.99, 7 x 10 format

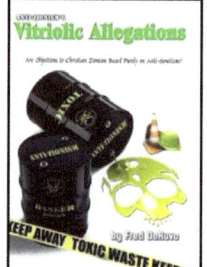

Anti-Zionism's Vitriolic Allegations
Those who believe God has with finality rejected Israel, see Christian Zionism as working *against* God. These same people, having rendered their verdict, offer nothing less than vitriolic rhetoric as a response. This book is a response to the virulent, dangerous and unchristian invective continually voiced by Anti-Zionists. TBA, 7 x 10 format

Between Weeks
It is often argued that the text in Daniel 9:24-27 is figurative, and therefore should automatically be taken allegorically. Others argue that there is no break between any of the weeks in this passage. 70 pages, $9.99, 7 x 10 format

Dispensationalism: Separating Fact from Fiction
There is a good deal of misinformation regarding Dispensationalism today. What is the truth? In a Q & A style, author Fred DeRuvo highlights the errant information, followed by a short explanation of the actual facts of the situation. TBA, 7 x 10 format

Interpreting the Bible Literally (Is Not As Confusing As It Sounds)
Unfortunately, too many Christians today are not aware that in order to study and interpret Scripture, certain tools (or methods) must be applied. It's like learning a foreign language, complete with idioms and other forms of figurative language. 235 pages, $10.99, 7 x 10 format

www.ingramcontent.com/pod-product-compliance
Lightning Source LLC
Chambersburg PA
CBHW041945110426
42744CB00027B/18